What Is a Gas?

by Jennifer Boothroyd

first step nonfiction

Lerner Publications Company · Minneapolis

All things are made of **matter.**

Matter is anything that takes up space.

There are three kinds of matter.

A **gas** is a kind of matter.

Air is a gas. It is hard to see some gases.

Steam is a hot gas. We can feel some gases.

Your breath is a gas. A gas
does not have its own shape.

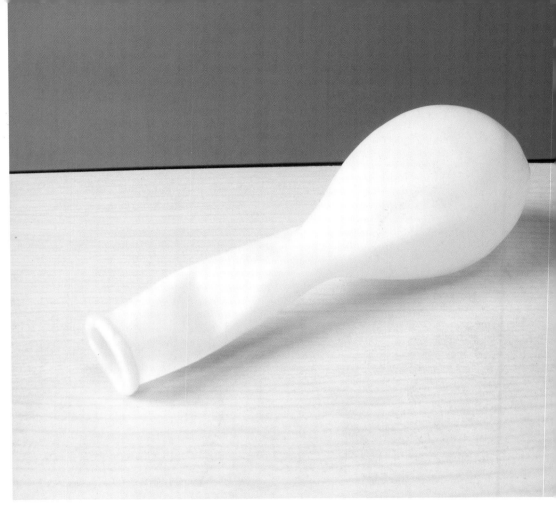

Gas can be put in a container.

The gas moves and fills the whole container.

It takes the shape of the container.

Gas in balloons can be many different shapes.

Cooling a gas can change it.

Cooling can change a gas to
a **liquid.**

Steam changes to water when it cools.

A cloud is made by cooling
a gas.

Look around. Where can you find gases?

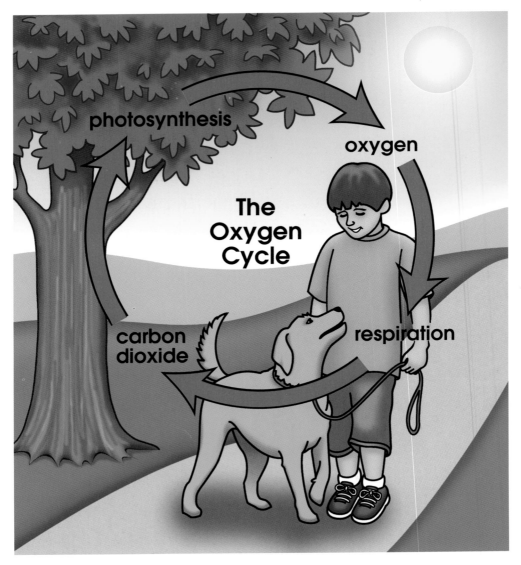

photosynthesis

oxygen

The
Oxygen
Cycle

carbon
dioxide

respiration

The Oxygen Cycle

Photosynthesis – Plants make their own food from sunlight, water, and a gas called carbon dioxide. When plants make their food, they also make a gas called oxygen, which goes out into the air.

Respiration – People and animals need oxygen to live. When people breathe in, they get oxygen from the air. When they breathe out, they put carbon dioxide into the air.

Fun Facts

 People and animals need oxygen to live. The air we breathe is made partly of oxygen. But it also contains other gases. Air is made mostly of nitrogen gas.

Carbon dioxide is the gas that makes bubbles in soda pop.

 Helium gas weighs less than air. That is why a balloon filled with helium floats.

Natural gas is found under the ground. People can use natural gas to cook their food, heat their homes, and dry their clothes.

Neon signs are made of glass tubes filled with neon gas. Electricity flows through the tubes and makes the gas glow.

The gas used in cars and trucks is actually a liquid. Here, the word gas is short for "gasoline."

Glossary

 gas – something that is not a liquid and takes the shape of its container

 liquid – something that flows

 matter – anything that takes up space

 steam – water that has become a gas

Index

The photographs in this book are used with the permission of: © Klaus Hackenberg/zefa/ CORBIS, front cover; © Stockbyte, pp. 2, 3, 22 (second from bottom); © Todd Strand/ Independent Picture Service, pp. 4 (top), 9, 10, 11; © Ryan McVay/Photodisc Green/Getty Images, pp. 4 (bottom), 8; PhotoDisc Royalty Free by Getty Images, pp. 4 (right), 5, 16, 17, 22 (top); © Royalty-Free/CORBIS, p. 6; © Rick Gayle/CORBIS, pp. 7, 22 (bottom); © Erica Johnson/Independent Picture Service, pp. 12, 15; © B MATHUR/Reuters/CORBIS, p. 13; © David De Lossy/Photodisc Green/Getty Images, pp. 14, 22 (second from top).

Illustration on page 18 by Laura Westlund/Independent Picture Service

Lerner Publications Company
A division of Lerner Publishing Group
241 First Avenue North
Minneapolis, MN 55401 U.S.A.

Website address: www.lernerbooks.com

Library of Congress Cataloging-in-Publication Data

Boothroyd, Jennifer, 1972–
        What is a gas? / by Jennifer Boothroyd.
           p.   cm. — (First step nonfiction)
        Includes index.
        ISBN-13: 978–0–8225–6837–7 (lib. bdg. : alk. paper)
        ISBN-10: 0–8225–6837–3 (lib. bdg. : alk. paper)
        1. Gases—Juvenile literature. I. Title. II. Series.
    QC161.2.B66 2007
    530.4'3—dc22   2006006303

Manufactured in the United States of America
1 2 3 4 5 6 – DP – 12 11 10 09 08 07